DATE DUE

Winston CHURCHILL

FIONA REYNOLDSON

Heinemann Library
Chicago, Illinois

Customer Service 888-454-2279

Visit our website at www.heinemannlibrary.com

Designed by AMR
Illustrated by Art Construction
Originated by Dot Gradations
Printed in China

05 04 03 02 01
10 9 8 7 6 5 4 3 2 1

Library of Congress Cataloging-in-Publication Data
Reynoldson, Fiona.
  Winston Churchill /c Fiona Reynoldson.
    p. cm. -- (Leading lives)
  Includes bibliographical references and index.
  ISBN 1-58810-163-0
  1. Churchill, Winston, Sir, 1874-1965--Juvenile literature. 2. Great
  Britain--Politics and government--20th century--Juvenile literature. 3.
  Prime ministers--Great Britain--Biography--Juvenile literature. [1.
  Churchill, Winston, Sir, 1874-1965. 2. Prime ministers.] I. Title. II.
  Series.

DA566.9.C5 R45 2001
941.084'092--dc21

                                                00-012842

Acknowledgments
The publishers would like to thank the following for permission to reproduce photographs:
AKG, pp. 9, 47, 48; Blenheim Palace, p. 4; Corbis, pp. 23, 24, 45, 49, 51; Hulton Getty, pp. 7, 10, 20, 25, 26, 30, 39, 40, 42, 44, 46, 52; Imperial War Museum, pp. 17, 28; PA Photos, p. 31; Peter Newark, p. 4; Popperfoto, pp. 12, 54; Rex, p. 8; Solo Syndication, pp. 34, 36.

Cover photograph reproduced with permission of Hulton Getty.

Our thanks to Christopher Gibb for his comments in the preparation of this book.

Every effort has been made to contact copyright holders of any material reproduced in this book. Any omissions will be rectified in subsequent printings if notice is given to the publishers.

Some words are shown in bold, **like this.** You can find out what they mean by looking in the glossary.

Contents

1 Churchill and the 20th Century

Lord and Lady Randolph Churchill were staying at Blenheim Palace in Oxfordshire, England in the autumn of 1874. Lady Randolph Churchill was just 20 years old and was expecting her first child. She gave birth to a son on November 30. He was named Winston Leonard Spencer Churchill.

Blenheim and the Churchills

Blenheim was the home of Winston Churchill's grandfather, the Seventh Duke of Marlborough. John Churchill, the First Duke of Marlborough, was the founder of the family fortune. He was the commander of the armies that defeated the French in battles at the beginning of the eighteenth century.

▲ Here is Blenheim Palace, Winston Churchill's birthplace. The palace dates back to 1704 and was a gift from Queen Anne to the First Duke of Marlborough.

Living through great changes

When Winston was born in 1874, there were no cars, let alone airplanes. Steam had only just taken over from sail as the power source running most ships. There was no electricity in houses, and few had running water indoors. Neither television nor radio had been invented, nor were there any telephones. Open coal fires heated houses. Rich people had indoor servants to carry the coal up and down the stairs and to do the washing, cooking, and cleaning. They had outdoor servants to look after the horses, carriages, and gardens.

By the time Winston died in 1965, the world had changed beyond recognition. Cars, airplanes, electricity, and all sorts of other inventions were taken for granted. Changes had come not only in material things, but also in people's attitudes. For instance, there was a far more widespread belief that ordinary people had a right to education, good housing, good healthcare, reasonable wages, and good working conditions. The rights of women had also changed dramatically. Winston Churchill not only lived through these changes, but played a part in creating them as well.

Winston Churchill and World War II

Churchill is best remembered now as Britain's leader during **World War II** (1939–45). He was over 60 years old when he became prime minister in May 1940. The German armies had swept through Western Europe, and it looked as though the defeat and conquest of Britain might follow. But Churchill was not daunted. It was his ability to see what needed to be done, to fight on, and to encourage everyone else to fight that was so valuable to Britain and the **Allies** at this difficult time.

2 Growing Up in Victorian England

The young Winston came from a very **aristocratic** and privileged background. His grandfather was the Seventh Duke of Marlborough, and his father was Lord Randolph Churchill, a Member of Parliament **(MP)** and ambitious politician of the time. His mother was the daughter of a wealthy businessman from New York. Winston's parents were generally too busy to pay much attention to their young son, but he had a devoted nanny named Mrs. Everest who traveled with them wherever they went.

Early school days

In 1880, Winston was six years old. His brother Jack was born that year, and two years later Winston was sent to boarding school. He did not do well. He was unhappy, partly because he was a difficult boy who refused to knuckle down to his work, and partly because he was beaten for his misbehavior by the headmaster. By the age of nine, he was ill with **pneumonia** and was sent to school at Brighton, by the sea. Winston was treated kindly there—the change brought improvements to his health and his schoolwork. He was good at French, history, and poetry, and he loved riding horses and swimming.

By the time he was thirteen years old, Winston's parents felt that he was ready to go to Harrow, a "public" or "independent" school, similar to what would be called a "private" school in the U.S., because it cost money to attend. For Christmas that year, his parents went to Russia, leaving Winston and Jack with their grandmother at Blenheim. His grandmother felt that Winston was clever and not really difficult; he just needed a firm hand. At his first school he had been accused of stealing sugar and stamping on the headmaster's hat, but all that seemed to be behind him now.

Lord Randolph Churchill

Lord Randolph Churchill, Winston's father, was the third son of the Duke of Marlborough. He went into politics and became the Member of Parliament for Woodstock. He became leader of the House of Commons and **Chancellor of the Exchequer** in 1886, when he was 37 years old. He lost out in a government argument and resigned in December that year. His political career was over at that point.

▶ *Winston's father, Lord Randolph Churchill, is pictured here.*

Going to school

Winston worked hard to pass the entrance examination into Harrow and went there in April 1888. However, once there, he was constantly late, lost his books, and was careless in his work. His father decided that he had better go into the army, as he did not think he was bright enough to become a lawyer. So Winston was moved into the army-bound class rather than the university one.

◀ *In 1900, the difficult life these poor boys had might have meant that they would have grown up to be as much as 4.7 in. (12 cm) shorter than boys in Winston's social class.*

Children in Victorian England

The life that Winston had as a boy was typical of children from wealthier homes in Victorian England. Children were expected to do as they were told and take up careers that their fathers decided upon. This was a world where obedience and duty were words that followed a child throughout childhood. But times were changing.

Changes in education

From the 1850s, public schools such as Rugby, Harrow, and Winchester began to improve. There were fewer incidences of bullying by older boys and less beating as punishment by teachers. A greater variety of education and sports was provided, but, of course, these schools were only for boys from wealthy families. Most girls from these families were still taught at home, although one or two good schools were opening for them as well.

For everyone else, an Education Act was passed in 1870. It set up state schools called Board Schools for children between ages five and ten. This followed laws that were passed to limit the number of hours children could work in factories. Even so, the gap between the rich and the poor was still very wide.

The rich and the poor growing up

The boys of wealthy parents looked forward to careers in law, the church, in politics, or as officers in the army or navy. Some of them had enough money to never have to work at all. At the other end of the social scale, children from Board Schools could only look ahead to jobs as laborers and servants. They were less healthy and they and their parents worked long hours, often in poor working conditions in coal mines or noisy, dusty factories. If they lost their jobs, they faced poverty. There were no **welfare systems** to pay them wages if they were sick, or **pensions** when they were old. On average, a rich boy like Winston could expect to be as much as 4.7 inches (12 centimeters) taller than a poor boy of the same age, due to the differences in the amount and **nutrition**

of the food they ate. These differences had not yet fully changed by the time Winston was in his thirties, but they were changing, and he was one of the people who started to make this happen.

◀ *This is Winston Churchill as a boy in about 1880.*

9

3 Into the Army

Although Churchill saw very little of his father, he idolized him and was devastated by his death in 1895. That year, Churchill had another blow when his much-loved nanny, Mrs. Everest, died. He was with her at the end and made all the arrangements for her funeral himself. Churchill was twenty years old. He had spent three years training to be a soldier at the Royal Military Academy at Sandhurst in Buckinghamshire. He had done well, graduating 20th in a class of 130. Now he was in a cavalry regiment, the 4th Hussars, in charge of 30 men, overseeing their daily duties and drilling.

◀ Churchill was photographed here as a lieutenant in the army in 1896.

The army and journalism

Churchill was already fascinated by politics and had discovered that he had a flair for journalism. While he was still in the cavalry, he went with a friend to the United States and then on to Cuba, where he had been asked to report on the fighting there. At the same time, he wrote articles for a newspaper, *The Daily Graphic*. This visit to Cuba is one of the first examples of Churchill's ability to persuade people to let him do things. It was not every young soldier who could persuade the British Director of Military Intelligence to let him report on a war in Cuba. Nor could every young man persuade a large newspaper to accept his articles. In both cases, Churchill used his connections through his famous father, but he had the initiative and the talent to carry out those jobs. For the rest of his life, most of his income came from his work as a writer and **journalist.**

Churchill's lisp

Churchill came home on leave in 1897 and went to see a doctor in London about his lisp. He pronounced "s" as "sh." Nothing was found to be wrong, but the lisp never went away. Despite this, he made his first political speech during his leave and later became a great **orator** in the House of Commons.

The trip to Cuba fired up his restless spirit. No sooner was he back in England than he was trying (through his mother's influence) to get to the center of action in Egypt or South Africa. This time, Churchill did not get his way, and he was sent instead to India, where he complained that he was bored. He started reading books about history, **philosophy,** and **economics.** He grew roses, collected butterflies, and started writing a novel.

At this time, India was part of the **British Empire,** which Churchill supported strongly. The people of India were beginning to demand more independence, but, in 1897, the British were still running the country with all the privileges that involved. When Churchill was in India, he enjoyed many of these privileges. He lived the easy life of a British officer. He shared a large bungalow with two other officer friends. Each man had a butler to oversee his household needs and the stables. In addition, each man had two servants to look after his clothes, and several grooms to look after his horses. They shared two gardeners, four washerwomen, and a watchman. The work of an officer was not very taxing if things were peaceful, so Churchill had plenty of time for reading, writing, and playing polo, which he enjoyed very much. However, he did not like an inactive life and constantly looked around for more action.

◀ These colonials, like many British officers in India, led a privileged life.

▲ This is a map of British India in 1897.

The Northwest Frontier

The young Churchill had once pestered his commander, General Sir Bindon Blood, to agree that if he ever commanded another expedition to the frontier between India and Afghanistan, he would let Churchill go with him. In 1897, Afghan tribesmen rebelled on the frontier. The general had no room on his staff, but suggested that Churchill get himself taken on as a **war correspondent** by one of the big newspapers. Churchill got his mother to persuade the *Daily Telegraph* newspaper to publish his letters from the battle area. With everything sorted out, he set off on the 5-day, 2,000-mile (3,200-kilometer) journey from his base in Bangalore to the frontier.

At the front

More than 50,000 British and Indian soldiers had been sent to fight the Afghan tribesmen. When Churchill arrived in September, he was attached to the second brigade of the Malakand Field Force, which had just been ordered into action. Although Churchill had reached the Northwest Frontier as a **journalist,** when he got there, General Blood kept to his early promise and took him on as a soldier.

Churchill was in his element. On September 16, he went out with 1,300 cavalry and an Indian infantry regiment. Fifty British and Indian men were killed and one hundred wounded. He and another officer carried back a wounded Indian. Churchill was mentioned in **dispatches** for the courage he had shown. However, as much as he loved the glory and the excitement, Churchill was upset by the deaths he had seen.

He was in the thick of fighting twice more that week, sometimes under fire for five hours at a time. He showed not only courage, but he also came to believe that he was meant to survive. In one of his letters to his mother he wrote: "I rode on my grey pony all along the skirmish line when everyone else was lying down in cover." Even he admitted this was possibly foolish.

General Blood was impressed with his enthusiasm and courage. Writing to a fellow officer, he predicted the young Churchill would be awarded medals for his bravery, saying: "He will have the **VC** or the **DSO**." General Blood failed to mention, however, what Churchill's mother may have thought: that Churchill's brave but foolhardy behavior might kill him before he could receive his medal!

Letters to the *Daily Telegraph*

Meanwhile, Churchill was sending letters back to London, to the *Daily Telegraph*. The newspaper published them, but without giving his name, only saying they were "from a young officer." Since Churchill wanted to be better known as a journalist and a man in public life, he was annoyed that his reports were anonymous. At the same time, he was writing reports for an Indian newspaper, and by the end of his time on the frontier, he had decided to write a book about the campaign on the frontier.

Fierce fighting

The fighting on the Northwest Frontier was fierce. Both sides regularly killed the enemy's wounded. Churchill won medals and gloried in the publicity, but there was a more thoughtful side to his character, too. He wrote that he wished he could *"come to the conclusion that all this barbarity—all these losses . . . had resulted in a permanent settlement."*

5 | The Battle of Omdurman

Churchill wrote his book about the Northwest Frontier and called it *The Story of the Malakand Field Force*. Its publication brought him some much-needed money, and the attention of the prime minister, Lord Salisbury, who had known Churchill's father well. Churchill asked Salisbury to help him get to the Sudan. In fact, he asked everyone he knew who had any influence to help him get there as part of the army under the command of Lord Kitchener.

Battle and victory

Churchill left London on July 27, 1898, to join the 21st Lancers, and a month later he was part of Kitchener's 25,000-man army. This army was closing in on Omdurman, where the enemy, the rebel Egyptians, was holding out against the British. On September 1, Churchill acted as a scout, reporting the numbers and position of the enemy to Kitchener. He stood on a small hill and watched enemy soldiers advancing by the thousands. The next day, Kitchener ordered a cavalry charge as part of his attack at what became known as the Battle of Omdurman. This was to be one of the last cavalry charges ever made by the British army. British soldiers used guns against an enemy largely equipped with spears, although a few also had guns. For Churchill, the most dangerous moment came after the charge, as he turned back and was nearly shot by two enemy riflemen. As the Lancers regrouped, they were pulled back to help the infantry. The enemy retreated, and by mid-morning the infantry was advancing toward Khartoum.

The excitement of the fighting and victory were tempered for Churchill by the loss of friends and by seeing the killing of many of the enemy wounded. This killing was something for which he criticized Kitchener in a book he wrote about the campaign, called *The River War*. The book was published in

1899 and infuriated Kitchener. He had not wanted Churchill on his campaign, knowing that he was a **journalist.** As far as he was concerned, this proved he had been right.

Lord Kitchener

Lord Kitchener was a successful soldier who became a field marshal. He made his name fighting in various parts of the **British Empire** and then as a governor and administrator. He was both energetic and thorough. At the outbreak of **World War I,** he became Secretary of State for War and organized the British Army. He died when the ship he was traveling on to Russia in June 1916 hit a German mine.

► *This poster, showing Kitchener calling Britons to join the army, became famous in his time, and is still well recognized today.*

Although he enjoyed the excitement of military adventures, Churchill wanted to make a career in politics. He wanted to follow in the footsteps of his father. However, first there were more adventures to come.

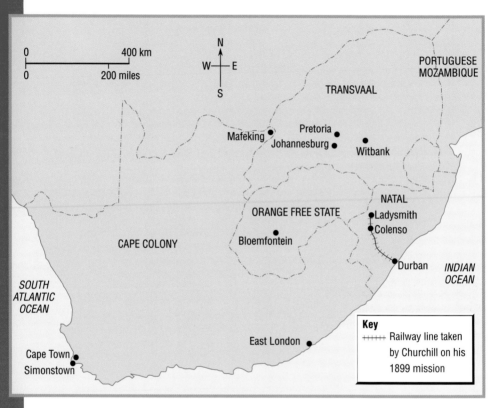

▲ This map shows South Africa from 1899 to 1900.

The first white settlers in South Africa were Dutch people. They were called **Boers.** Britain began to take over control of South Africa from the beginning of the nineteenth century, and there were clashes between the Boers and the British. These came to a head in 1899, and the two sides moved toward war. Churchill contacted the *Daily Mail* and was taken on as their **war correspondent.** By this time, he was a better-known

journalist and was paid the high rate of £1,000 for a four-month contract—the equivalent of over $58,000 today. After a seventeen-day voyage by ship, Churchill was in South Africa. It was October 31, 1899.

Traveling by train and boat, Churchill was soon near the front line of the fighting. A week or so later, Captain Haldane, who had known Churchill in India, was ordered to take an armored train into the fighting area. His orders were to find out more about what the Boers were up to. Haldane asked Churchill to join them.

Their train departed at 5:10 A.M. with 150 men on board. Two hours later, it was in frontline country and ran into the enemy. The train was **shelled.** The engine driver, hoping to outrun the ambush, took off at full steam. The train gathered speed downhill, but less than one mile (two kilometers) later it ran into a boulder on the line, which derailed the trucks that were being pushed in front of the engine. The train was stuck. Later Haldane wrote: "Churchill immediately offered his services and, knowing how thoroughly I could rely on him, I gladly accepted them, and undertook to keep down the enemy's fire while he endeavoured to clear the line."

A resourceful journalist

Churchill and another journalist caught a train to a town called Ladysmith, which was likely to be captured by the Boers. They could not get closer than 60 miles (96 kilometers), so Churchill rented a train and they got as far as Colenso. Here they were fired at, and the train went no further. They set up their tents in the railway yard so they could stay near the action.

Bravery and capture

Churchill organized the soldiers to clear the derailed trucks away by hand, and had the engine driver push some of the wreckage away with the engine. They were under fire the whole time. Four men were killed and thirty wounded. One of the wounded was the engine driver. After an hour or so, they partially cleared the line and Churchill took the train, picking up the wounded and taking them to safety a short distance away. Then he walked back to help Haldane and the 50 remaining soldiers fight. He never made it. Some Boer horsemen caught him, and when he reached for his pistol he realized that he had left it on the engine when he was helping to clear the track. There was nothing to do but surrender.

▲ *Churchill is pictured here on the right, after being captured by the Boers.*

Prison and escape

Churchill was put in prison together with Haldane, who had also been forced to surrender. They decided to try and escape by night. When they made the attempt, Churchill got over the wall safely, but a sentry stopped Haldane. Churchill was on his own. He also realized that he had no compass, no map, and no money. He had to travel 300 miles (500 kilometers) to get out of Boer land, and he could not speak the language. He strolled off down the street, humming a tune, heading for the railway station. Before reaching the station, he jumped onto a slow-moving goods train and hid in the empty coal wagon.

The train traveled through the night, and at dawn he jumped out near a small mining town. That night, hungry and thirsty, he decided he would have to seek help. By a stroke of luck, he knocked on the door of a house where British people lived. A reward for capturing Churchill—dead or alive—had already been announced by the Boers, so the family agreed to hide him in the coal mine. A few days later they hid him on a coal train, heading for the border. Two days later he was free, and he became famous for his daring escape.

A wanted man

"Englishman 25 years old, about 5 feet 8 inches tall, average build, walks with a slight stoop, pale appearance, red brown hair, almost invisible small moustache, speaks through the nose, cannot pronounce the letter 's,' cannot speak Dutch, has last been seen in a brown suit of clothes. Reward—£25.00 dead or alive."

(Description of Churchill from the Boer "Wanted" poster)

7 The New MP

By July 1900, Churchill was back in England. He was a national hero and several **constituencies** wanted him to run as their Member of Parliament **(MP).** He agreed to run for Oldham, in the north of England, where 10,000 people turned out to greet him, cheering and waving flags. In the **general election,** in October, he became their MP. Churchill was just 25 years old—he had already done more than many people twice his age and had now achieved his ambition of being an MP. He was following in his father's footsteps and was earning a good living. His reports from the fighting in South Africa had earned him the equivalent of about $130,000 (£90,000) today. He was publishing a fifth book and setting up a new career as a lecturer in Britain and the United States.

In Parliament

Churchill made his **maiden speech** on February 28, 1901. He spoke about the war in South Africa and, despite his lisp, impressed the other MPs and the newspapers with his style, self-assurance, and good judgement. He was all set for a great career in the **Conservative Party.** However, he did not agree with his party on several points. The most important were the questions of **free trade** and **protectionism** and the amount the government spent on defense.

Free trade and protectionism

Free trade is an economic system in which a country does not have any duties or taxes on **imported** or **exported** goods. Protectionism is an economic system in which a country puts duties or taxes on goods being imported. The reason for protection is to make sure the home country's industries survive. For instance, if Britain had many factories making sewing machines, and another country could make them much more cheaply, the British government might put a duty or tax on any foreign sewing machines being imported into Britain to make sure they could not be sold more cheaply than British ones. If they did not do this, people making sewing machines in Britain might lose their jobs. Protectionism was a Conservative Party policy in 1901. Churchill felt strongly that Britain had been a free trade country for a long time and free trade meant more trade for everyone—protectionism would reduce trading, and this would harm Britain in the long run.

▲ This is a formal photograph of Churchill as a young MP in 1900.

After four years in the **Conservative Party,** Churchill was becoming more and more unpopular due to his views on **free trade.** On May 31, 1904, he left the Conservatives and joined the **Liberal Party.** Two years later, in 1906, the Liberal Party came to power, having won a big majority in the House of Commons. Here was Churchill's chance. He became a junior minister with responsibility for the **colonies.** During this time he negotiated a settlement in South Africa, where he wanted justice for the **Boers,** and held out against any vindictive treatment of a defeated enemy.

Reform

After working in the colonial office in 1905, Churchill became president of the Board of Trade in 1908, and then **Home Secretary** in 1910. It was at this time that he turned his mind to **social reform.** Much of his work was with Prime Minister David Lloyd George, who also passionately wanted to improve the lives of poorer and older people. This meant that other people would have to be charged more in taxes to pay for **pensions** and other reforms. Lloyd George brought in a **budget,** which became known as the "People's Budget." In it, he suggested charging a bigger tax on all incomes over $7,200 (£5,000) a year, increasing **death duties,** and introducing taxes on land, automobiles, and gasoline. There was a huge outcry against these plans from wealthy people.

◀ *Prime Minister Lloyd George and Winston Churchill are walking in London in 1910.*

The Liberal government also had to face the problem of Ireland at this time. The Irish MPs supported the government in its battle to get the House of Commons and the House of Lords to agree to find the money for the reforms. However, in return, the Irish wanted **Home Rule.** They wanted as much independence from Britain as possible.

Another problem was that Britain was worried about the power of Germany. Germany was building a large navy, and Britain, largely a naval power, felt the need to build more warships to counteract any German threat. These warships cost a great deal of money, which had to be found from taxes as well.

Getting married

In the midst of all his government work, Churchill got married. He had met Clementine Hozier a few years before they married in 1908. She was 23 and he was 33. They made their home in London and had five children together, of whom one, Marigold, died of **meningitis** at the age of two and a half in 1921.

▲ *Churchill is shown here with his fiancée Clementine Hozier in 1908.*

The years between 1908 and 1914 were busy ones for Churchill. As **Home Secretary,** he was dealing with many strikes as workers fought for better working conditions and better pay. There was also unrest as women campaigned to get the vote, and there was the continual issue of Ireland.

The most dramatic moment of Churchill's time as Home Secretary was the "Sidney Street Siege" of 1911. Three policemen in London were killed while chasing a gang of burglars who then barricaded themselves in a house on Sidney Street. After the gang killed another policeman, Churchill ordered troops to move in and went to see what was happening for himself. Two members of the gang died when the house caught fire, and the third was never caught.

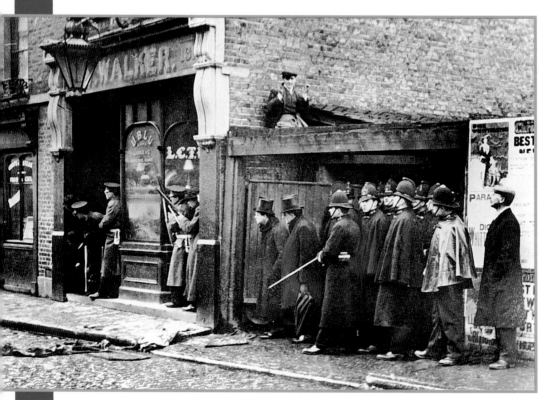

▲ This photograph is from the Sidney Street Siege. Churchill is in the center of the photograph, at the front of the group of observers.

Churchill was criticized because many people thought he had interfered with the work of the police during the siege. He had made many enemies, particularly from the **Conservative Party** that he had left, and which was ready to criticize anything he did.

First Lord of the Admiralty

Later, in 1911, Churchill changed jobs to become First Lord of the Admiralty, which made him responsible for the navy. Since many people were increasingly worried about the growth of the German army and navy, Churchill was interested in improving the navy. In his usual energetic way, he dealt with everything from getting a pay raise for ordinary sailors to introducing new oil-fired ships to replace the old coal-burning ones.

Churchill was busy at the Admiralty and happy at home. He had a daughter, Diana, and a son, Randolph. He enjoyed his work and started to learn to fly, much to Clementine's dismay. She pointed out that it was a very dangerous new sport. When his flying instructor was killed, Churchill agreed to give it up. But serious trouble, on a far larger scale, was brewing when Britain was drawn into a war in Europe in 1914.

Causes of World War I

Before **World War I,** the great powers were divided into two **alliances.** The main powers were Germany and Austria-Hungary on one side, and Russia and France on the other, with Britain friendly towards France.

In July 1914, a Serbian shot the Archduke Franz Ferdinand, who was heir to the Austro-Hungarian Empire. This led to war between Serbia and Austria-Hungary. Russia supported the Serbs. Germany supported Austria-Hungary. France was an **ally** of Russia and, finally, Britain was drawn in when Germany invaded Belgium, whose frontiers had been guaranteed protection by Britain.

10 Disgrace and Comeback

▲ *These soldiers are fighting on the Western Front in 1915.*

When war came, Churchill wanted action. He soon saw, together with Lloyd George and others, that the fighting on the **Western Front** had reached a stalemate—a point at which no one could win. Soldiers who tried to attack the enemy's **trenches** were being stopped by barbed wire and taken down by machine guns and artillery.

The first tanks and Gallipoli

In 1915, Churchill met Major Thomas Hetherington, who had invented an armored vehicle like a strong metal box. It could carry guns and soldiers across rough ground, and in this way break through the trenches. Churchill saw this as a way out of the stalemate and ordered trials of this vehicle, later called the tank. He also suggested that they attack much further south, where there were no trenches. He suggested attacking Germany's **ally** Turkey at a place called Gallipoli on the Straits of Dardanelles. The attack was launched in 1915, and was a terribly costly failure in terms of men and resources. Churchill thought the navy could do the job, using outdated battleships to destroy the Turkish forts, without the army being involved—in this he was wrong. Although Churchill was only partly to blame, he took all the responsibility and was forced to resign from the government. His enemies were delighted. Churchill was disgraced, and it looked as though his career was over for good.

Back to being a soldier

With no job to do, Churchill rejoined the army as a soldier on the front line. He spent the next three months in the trenches in Belgium as a lieutenant-colonel with the 6th Royal Scots Fusiliers. He paid attention to everything from exterminating lice among the soldiers to campaigning for **conscription.**

He hoped to come back into politics. The war was dragging on and a new government was formed. It was a **coalition** of all the parties. However, this meant that although Churchill's old friend David Lloyd George was prime minister, there would be **Conservative Party** members in the government too. They still refused to have anything to do with Churchill.

Nevertheless, Churchill was famous and very capable. It was difficult to leave him out. In July 1917, Lloyd George asked him to join the government, in charge of **munitions.** He put all his energy into this until the end of the war.

11 After the War

World War I ended on November 11, 1918. Clementine was expecting their fourth child and she came to London to be with Churchill as the news of victory came through. The streets swarmed with people celebrating. The long war was over. But how would the peace hold out?

▲ *These people are celebrating the end of WW I in London on Armistice Day, November 11, 1918.*

The Treaty of Versailles

The Treaty of Versailles, signed by Germany, Britain, and France, set out the conditions of peace for Germany. Among other things, it laid the blame for the war on Germany and stated that Germany should pay for the damage caused. France, where much of the fighting had taken place, especially wanted Germany to pay. Lloyd George and Churchill were among the few people who did not want harsh terms. They preferred to raise money by taxing the people who had made huge profits from making war goods—ammunition, army boots, and other supplies.

FOR DETAILS ON KEY PEOPLE OF CHURCHILL'S TIME, SEE PAGE 58.

Changing parties again

Sorting out treaties was not the only problem. Churchill remained in Lloyd George's government until 1922, dealing with Russia, where a **civil war** was following the revolution of 1917. Churchill always feared **Communism,** so he was strongly against the **Bolshevik Party,** led by Lenin in Russia. But Russia was too large for any outsiders to have much influence.

In Ireland, Churchill was more **conciliatory,** and looked for ways to bring about an agreement. Soon, however, the old wartime government was out of power and the new **Labour Party** was in power for the first time. Although he had strived for better conditions for working people, such as old-age **pensions,** Churchill was not happy with the Labour Party, mainly because of his fear that they would give working people too much power. The **Liberal Party** was in decline, so he moved further toward the **Conservative Party,** which he had left years before. In 1924, when the Conservatives regained power, Churchill rejoined and became **Chancellor of the Exchequer.**

12 The General Strike

As **Chancellor of the Exchequer,** Churchill, relying heavily on his advisers, returned Britain to the **Gold Standard.** This made British exports more expensive for other countries to buy, and so led to more unemployment in Britain. The situation deteriorated further when increasing economic problems in the United States led to the Wall Street **stock market** crash in 1929. The U.S. stock market crash affected other countries in the world and unemployment increased even more. The period of the 1930s became known as the Great Depression. Churchill and the Conservatives would be out of power by that time, but they had their share of problems to deal with before then.

The General Strike

The **General Strike** of 1926 began because coal miners were in dispute with the mine owners, principally because the owners wished to impose longer hours and lower wages on workers. When the miners refused to accept these terms, they were locked out of the pits. This led to a strike of all workers in Britain—the General Strike.

Without newspaper printers, there was no news. So Churchill was put in charge of running a government newspaper called *The British Gazette*. Articles in this newspaper clearly showed Churchill's dislike of **Communism.** He talked of links between the Russian Communists and the striking workers. But it was probably his fear of a breakdown in law and order that made him want the strike put down so firmly. His strength of feeling on this issue alienated Churchill from many working-class people for the rest of his life. However, as soon as the General Strike was over, the Prime Minister chose him to take charge of the negotiations with the coal miners, as he was still known as a fair negotiator.

The wilderness years

Churchill was in the government until 1929, when the **general election** went against the Conservatives. For the next ten years he was out of government and generally out of favor. These years came to be called his "wilderness years." He was openly against the **Conservative Party's** policy on the future of India, and was accused of letting down his party once again. He also supported the future king, Edward VIII, who was forced to **abdicate** the throne because he wanted to marry a divorcée. Churchill felt that his political life was finished.

Chartwell

In 1922, the Churchills had their fifth child, a daughter named Mary. On the same day, Churchill bought Chartwell Manor in Kent. He took great delight in this new house, which he renovated, and in which he and Clementine were to live for the next 40 years.

▶ *This is the drawing room at Chartwell.*

13 Toward World War II

Throughout the 1930s, it seemed as though Churchill's reputation for being clever but rash and impossible to work with was going to stay with him and keep him out of politics for the rest of his life. After all, he had changed political parties twice, so could he really be trusted by his colleagues? In Churchill's defense, he made these decisions because he never put party before principle. If he thought something was right, then he stood by it regardless of his party's views.

As the 1930s progressed, it seemed to him increasingly important to oppose the growing power of the **Nazi** Party in Germany and its leader, Adolf Hitler. Hitler had come to power promising to make Germany powerful and rich again. In a gesture to keep the peace and from a feeling that Germany should be fairly treated, some European powers, including Britain, agreed to let Germany have land back that had been taken away after **World War I.** This policy was called appeasement. Unfortunately, it carried with it the risk of Hitler wanting more and more land, and of Germany growing ever more powerful. The question was, at whose expense would Germany's growth in power come? Germany could only grow more powerful at the expense of the countries around Germany and of Europe in general.

◀ *This cartoon comments on the fact that many people thought Churchill had a "bee in his bonnet" about (was obsessed by) Germany building airplanes.*

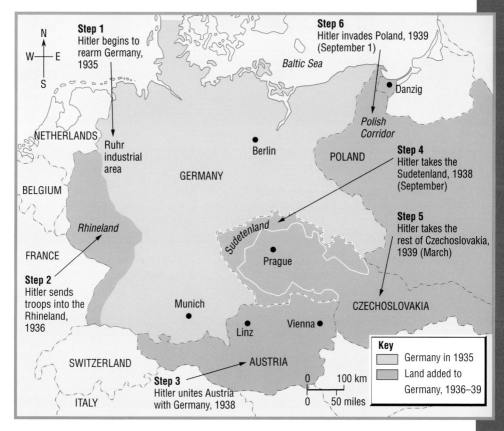

The following labels appear on the map:

Step 1 Hitler begins to rearm Germany, 1935

Step 6 Hitler invades Poland, 1939 (September 1)

Baltic Sea

Danzig

Polish Corridor

NETHERLANDS

Ruhr industrial area

Berlin

POLAND

Step 4 Hitler takes the Sudetenland, 1938 (September)

GERMANY

BELGIUM

Rhineland

Sudetenland

Step 5 Hitler takes the rest of Czechoslovakia, 1939 (March)

FRANCE

Prague

Step 2 Hitler sends troops into the Rhineland, 1936

Munich

CZECHOSLOVAKIA

Linz

Vienna

SWITZERLAND

AUSTRIA

0   100 km

0   50 miles

Step 3 Hitler unites Austria with Germany, 1938

ITALY

Key
Germany in 1935
Land added to Germany, 1936–39

N W E S

▲ *This map illustrates the steps leading to World War II, 1935–39.*

Churchill repeatedly warned the British about German ambitions and the growth of the German armed forces. He wrote articles for *The Evening Standard*, a newspaper with a circulation of three million in London alone, and he made speeches. By late 1937, he was warning that the next year would see "Germany relatively stronger to the British Air Force and to the French Army."

Meanwhile, the British government, led by Prime Minister Neville Chamberlain, tried to keep the peace with Hitler, but there was always some new demand. On September 1, 1939, the German army marched into Poland. At this point, Britain and France decided to take a stand against Hitler's Germany. Britain declared war on September 3, 1939.

14 War Is Declared

▲ *This cartoon shows the determination of Churchill (front left) and other government members to fight Germany.*

As soon as war was declared, Churchill was appointed First Lord of the Admiralty, in charge of the navy again. Not even his greatest critics doubted his energy and ability to get things done—and this energy seemed undiminished despite the fact that on November 30, 1939, he turned 65 years old and had been in politics for 40 years.

By May 1940, Germany had invaded Norway. The threat to Western Europe was growing. Both Parliament and the people of Britain were uneasy about the war, and this led to the fall of the government under Neville Chamberlain. Churchill, who had repeatedly warned that war would come, was not the first choice to be prime minister at the head of a new **coalition** government. Members of the **Labour Party** were extremely suspicious of him at first. They only accepted him when another candidate, Lord Halifax, declined the appointment. Churchill was relieved. He wrote: "At last I had authority to give directions over the whole scene . . . all my past life had been but a preparation for this hour and for this trial . . . and I was sure I would not fail."

Blood, toil, tears, and sweat

Almost at the same time as Churchill became prime minister, Hitler's armies moved into Holland, Belgium, and Luxembourg. Then the German armies swept on toward France. If France were defeated, what would Britain do? Churchill's confidence, determination, and oratory laid low the doubts. Most people felt he was the only person who could lead the country against Germany and **Nazi** ambitions.

Churchill—a rousing orator

"I have nothing to offer but blood, toil, tears, and sweat . . . You ask what is our policy? I can say: it is to wage war, by sea, land, and air with all the might and with all the strength that God can give us; to wage war against a monstrous tyranny, never surpassed in the dark, lamentable catalog of human crime. That is our policy. You ask, what is our aim? I can answer in one word: victory, victory at all costs, victory in spite of all terror, victory, however long and hard the road may be; for without victory there is no survival."

(An excerpt from a speech Churchill made in the House of Commons in 1940)

15 His Finest Hour

At dawn on May 10, 1940, German troops invaded Denmark and Holland, and attacked Belgium. By May 16, German troops had isolated the Maginot Line, a group of ports important for the defense of France. The French army was forced to retreat. The British Expeditionary Force pulled back from Belgium at the same time. By May 21, the Germans had chased the British and part of the French army to the coast at Dunkirk and trapped them.

Churchill was in contact with President Franklin Roosevelt, seeking American help. He also flew to France to encourage the French to keep fighting. Neither strategy worked at this time. On May 26, the order was given to **evacuate** as many of the trapped British and French soldiers as possible back to Britain. Those British soldiers who were still in Calais, near Dunkirk, were to hold the Germans back for as long as possible. They would not be evacuated. It was a grim decision to make. At dinner that night, Churchill ate very little. He told Eden, the Minister of War, that he felt "physically sick."

Dunkirk

The evacuation started on May 27. Some soldiers were rescued from the port of Dunkirk, others from the broad sandy beaches. No one thought that more than a few thousand could ever be saved. Yet, as the days passed and the weather held, more and more men were picked up and ferried back to England. By June 4, 224,318 British and 111,172 French soldiers had been rescued. Churchill spoke in the House of Commons of a "miracle of deliverance," but he warned "wars are not won by evacuations."

▲ *These French men are being rescued from a sinking raft on the way back from Dunkirk.*

Fighting talk

"Even though large tracts of Europe and many old and famous states have fallen or may fall into the grip of the **Gestapo** *and the odious apparatus of* **Nazi** *rule, we shall not flag or fail. We shall go on to the end. We shall fight in France, we shall fight on the seas and oceans, we shall fight with growing confidence and growing strength in the air, we shall defend our island, whatever the cost may be. We shall fight on the beaches, we shall fight on the landing grounds, we shall fight in the fields and in the streets, we shall fight in the hills; we shall never surrender."*

(Excerpt from Churchill's speech on June 4, 1940, following the evacuation of Dunkirk)

LET US
GO FORWARD
TOGETHER"

◀ *This is a poster of Winston Churchill during World War II. It was available for sale at the government Stationery Office in London.*

Britain destroys the French fleet

By the middle of June, France was overrun and had surrendered to Germany. The surrender included the French fleet. A large number of these ships were in North Africa and, in order to stop them from being taken by the Germans and used against Britain, Churchill ordered the British navy to sink them. Over 1,200 French sailors were killed and Franco-British relations were severely undermined. However, as Churchill pointed out, this was no time for "doubt or weakness." Indeed, within a few days, the sinking became a symbol for British ruthlessness and determination, sending a clear message to the United States, and Germany, that Britain would fight on. When Churchill announced this in the House of Commons, he was cheered.

Peace?

However, there was less and less to cheer about. France, Belgium, Holland, Luxembourg, Denmark, and Norway had fallen. The U.S. showed no signs of entering the war, and the **Soviet Union** had a pact with Hitler. It is clear now that some senior British ministers might have contemplated coming to an agreement with Hitler as well, if this had guaranteed all of Britain's rights and powers. But Hitler's proposals for peace were unacceptable. Would Hitler force Britain out of the war by invading the British Isles? The German navy would not go in unless the British air force (RAF) was destroyed first. Thus began the Battle of Britain in July 1940.

The Battle of Britain

From the middle of July 1940, German bombers and fighters flew over Britain to attack airfields and planes. The RAF (Royal Air Force) sent Hurricane and Spitfire fighter planes to intercept the enemy. Many fights followed in the long, hot summer days. On August 16, Churchill visited the operations room of RAF Fighter Command at Uxbridge. Almost all of Britain's available fighters were in the air that day, engaged in fierce fighting with the German air force. When Churchill left, he said to his secretary: "Don't speak to me; I have never been so moved. . . Never in the field of human conflict has so much been owed by so many to so few." A few days later, he used the same words in a speech to the House of Commons. The words, like many of his speeches, caught the mood and emotion of the time, as the Battle of Britain moved to a climax.

▶ *This painting is of RAF Spitfires and German aircraft during the Battle of Britain.*

Turning point

On September 15, Churchill was again at Uxbridge. From the operations room he could see that every available Spitfire and Hurricane was already in the air. When another wave of German planes crossed the coast, there were no more British planes to send out to challenge them. Churchill drove away, exhausted. However, by that evening, the German air force had lost 59 of their bombers. They could not afford to continue with such big losses. Many people saw this as the turning point of the Battle of Britain.

The Blitz

That winter, Hitler began bombing London and many other British cities by night. This became known as the blitz. Despite the bombing, Churchill and his wife stayed in London. They moved from 10 Downing Street to a set of rooms overlooking St. James's Park. The rooms were strengthened with steel girders and there were steel shutters on the windows. Below ground level were specially fortified rooms known as the Cabinet War Rooms, where the main government ministers met throughout the war. Churchill had a bed there in case the bombing became really bad, but he was not easily intimidated. In all, he only slept below ground for three nights.

◄ Churchill visits an area of Manchester that had been bombed in the Blitz.

In June 1941, Hitler turned away from Western Europe and invaded the **Soviet Union,** breaking the pact the **Nazis** had made with the Soviets. As soon as the news reached London, many in the government thought that the Soviets would be quickly defeated. But Churchill offered odds of 500 to 1 that the Soviet Union would not only still be fighting, but winning, two years on. Despite his dislike of **Communism,** he understood that British friendship with the Soviet Union was essential at that time. He offered to help the Soviet Union with supplies and to share some information Britain had gained from code breaking.

Code breaking at Bletchley

From early in the war, a group of British **cryptographers** had been gathered together at a top-secret site called Bletchley. They had managed to break the German code, using a machine called the **Enigma machine.** This meant that the British knew what the German armed forces were planning to do. This had already proved extremely useful to Britain; now Churchill was prepared to use it to help Stalin, the leader of the Soviet Union. On June 27, 1941, the cryptographers at Bletchley broke the Enigma code being used by the Germans on the Eastern Front, where they were fighting the Soviet Union. Churchill was careful not to reveal to Stalin that the information came from code breaking. The fewer people who knew of this, the better.

Churchill and Roosevelt

Within a few months of Hitler's invasion of the Soviet Union, Churchill met President Roosevelt in Newfoundland, Canada. Although many people in the United States still wanted to stay out of a European war, Roosevelt was offering to help Britain by, among other things, sending American destroyers to escort convoys carrying supplies from the U.S. to Britain. Churchill felt that he had "established warm and deep personal relations" with Roosevelt, a connection he felt Britain sorely needed. He remarked later that the battle to bring food and war supplies across the Atlantic in the teeth of German attack by U-boats (German submarines) was the only part of the war that really terrified him. Britain could not have survived without this lifeline of support from the U.S. Churchill wanted more, however—he wanted the U.S. in the war. His wish was granted after December 7, 1941, the day when Japan, Germany's **ally,** attacked the American Pacific naval base at Pearl Harbor in Hawaii.

▲ *President Roosevelt and Winston Churchill meet on board a ship in the Atlantic in August 1941.*

17 The Tide Changes

With the U.S. coming into the war, Churchill knew that Germany and its **allies** would be defeated. But there was still a long way to go. On February 14, 1942, the British island of Singapore fell to the Japanese and thousands of British, Australian, and Indian soldiers were taken prisoner. It was a terrible blow. Another setback came when the Germans changed the **Enigma machine** and the British could not read the German secret codes for a year. Outwardly, Churchill was confident and determined to keep morale up. But his family saw a different picture. His daughter Mary wrote in her diary on February 27: "Papa is at a very low ebb. He is not too well physically, and he is worn down by the continuous pressure of events."

The strain of the war

The Japanese took more and more territory in the Far East. Churchill escaped to Chartwell for short breaks, but his work schedule was punishing and included a huge amount of traveling. As well as going to the U.S. to meet with Roosevelt, Churchill visited North Africa, because he wanted to fight the Germans there in order to take pressure off the Soviets. He also visited Stalin in the **Soviet Union.** Churchill was under such strain that he suffered heart trouble and, in 1943, he came down with **pneumonia** following a visit to North Africa.

▲ *Churchill works at his upright desk at Chartwell.*

▲ *Stalin and Churchill, leaders of Allied countries during World War II, are pictured here.*

By mid-1943, Churchill's spirits were lifted somewhat when North Africa was taken into Allied hands. The Allies were poised to invade Italy. This was good news for Stalin, who had been pressing for Britain and the U.S. to do something in the West in order to divert German soldiers away from the Eastern Front and take some pressure off the Soviets. The victory in North Africa, the landings in Italy, and the bombing of German cities all helped to ease the pressure on Stalin and the Soviet troops. Still, by far the greatest amount of fighting was taking place between the Soviet Union and the Germans, and Stalin wanted more action—a full-scale invasion of northern Europe by Britain and the U.S.

The turning point

The battle that turned the tide for Britain in North Africa was the British victory at El Alamein. Just after the news of the victory came through, Churchill made a broadcast on the radio. He declared that this victory was not the beginning of the end of the war, but was "the end of the beginning."

18 The End of the War

Throughout 1943, the **Allies** were building up to the moment when they would invade Europe. Hundreds of thousands of American and **Commonwealth** soldiers were gathered in Britain. By this time, the biggest contribution in the war, after the **Soviet Union,** was coming from the U.S. Churchill was well aware of this. He presided over a special government committee dealing with the invasion of Europe, but the Supreme Allied Commander in charge of the invasion was an American—General Eisenhower (see page 58). Churchill was very eager, as always, to be a part of the action. He wanted to go across the English Channel to France with the first wave of ships that were due to land in Normandy. His government colleagues were dismayed. They could not afford to lose the Prime Minister. The plan was dropped only when King George VI of England said he would like to go, and if he couldn't go then neither could Churchill.

D–Day, June 6, 1944

The first day of the invasion was June 6, 1944, when over 150,000 soldiers landed on five beaches in Normandy. This really was the "beginning of the end," although it was to be another eleven months before the Allies reached Berlin.

▼ *These U.S. troops are landing in Normandy on D-Day.*

◀ Churchill, Roosevelt, and Stalin met at Yalta in February 1945.

Even before the war was truly over, the "Big Three" (the Soviet Union, the U.S., and Britain) were discussing peace treaties. They met at Yalta in the Ukraine in February 1945. Agreements were reached among Stalin, Roosevelt, and Churchill. One of these agreements concerned holding **free elections** in Poland and all Eastern European countries, occupied at this time by the armies of the Soviet Union, who were advancing toward Germany. Stalin agreed to allow free elections and promised them soon. Roosevelt seemed to believe him, but Churchill was dubious, although he could not prove anything. Within a short space of time it was obvious that Stalin had no intention of sticking to his promise, and this was effectively the end of the Anglo-Soviet **alliance.** Churchill was aware that conflicts might arise—possibly with the Soviet Union itself.

A sad heart

". . . my heart is saddened by the tales of the masses of German women and children flying along the roads . . . before the advancing armies . . . . The misery of the whole world appals me, and I fear increasingly that new struggles may arise out of those we are successfully ending."

(Excerpt from a letter Churchill wrote to his wife in February 1945)

Victory in Europe

The war in Europe ended on May 8, 1945—"Victory in Europe" (VE) day. Churchill gave a broadcast on the radio and people listened, enthralled. Crowds took to the streets to celebrate, particularly in London. Churchill spoke in the House of Commons and appeared on a balcony outside one of the government buildings. He told the crowds below him: "This is your victory." "No," they shouted back, "it's yours."

FOR DETAILS ON KEY PEOPLE OF CHURCHILL'S TIME, SEE PAGE 58.

General election, July 1945

Churchill's contribution to winning the war was appreciated by the vast majority of people in Britain. But the war was over. A **general election** was held in July and, to his surprise, Churchill lost. A Labour government was voted in, with Clement Attlee as prime minister. Churchill was bitterly disappointed and hurt. He was obviously not the leader the British people wanted in peacetime. This was mainly because British people wanted to have a better life after the war—a national health service and a **welfare system,** better housing and employment. Most voters felt that the **Labour Party** would bring about more of these reforms than Churchill and the **Conservative Party.**

◀ *Churchill triumphs amid crowds, showing the "V for Victory" sign at the end of World War II.*

▲ *Churchill had taken up painting when his political career was at a low in 1915, and kept it up for the rest of his life. Here he is at his easel in 1945.*

Although the wartime **coalition** government that Churchill had led so successfully was voted out of office in the **general election** of 1945, Churchill himself kept his seat in the House of Commons by a good majority. He said, however, that he was "very lonely without a war." Many people, including his wife, thought that it was time for him to retire from politics altogether. Churchill was now 71 years old—but he could not give up, mainly because he was still fascinated by politics and the world of foreign affairs.

The Fulton Speech

In 1946, Churchill was asked to give a speech at the University of Missouri at Fulton in the United States. In this speech, he warned against the dangers of the spread of **Communism** in Eastern Europe under the control of Stalin and the **Soviet Union**: "From Stettin in the Baltic to Trieste in the Adriatic, an iron curtain has descended across the continent. Behind that line all the capitals of the ancient states of Central and Eastern Europe—Warsaw, Berlin, Prague, Vienna, Budapest, Bucharest, Sofia, all those famous cities and the populations around them, lie in the Soviet sphere." Churchill's phrase "the iron curtain" immediately caught the public's imagination and it came to symbolize the hostile divide between East and West as the period that became known as the **Cold War** took hold.

Prime minister again

The Labour government carried through many **social reforms,** such as bringing in the National Health Service, which meant everyone could have free medical treatment. However, by 1951, the Conservatives were voted back into power, with Churchill once more at the helm. Although there were still sometimes flashes of the old fire and leadership ability, Churchill was really too old to cope with the demands of being prime minister. He led his party and his country for another four years, until 1955, when he finally retired. He remained an **MP** until 1959, though increasing ill health meant that he rarely put in an appearance at the House of Commons. He died on January 24, 1965, at the age of 91.

Churchill was given a state funeral—the first **commoner** since the Duke of Wellington, in the mid-nineteenth century, to have been given such a tribute. Over 300,000 people filed past his coffin in Westminster Hall, and huge crowds lined the route of the funeral procession. In the eyes of many who had lived through **World War II,** he was the leader who had saved Britain. Was he really a great man, and what was his legacy?

Social reform

Churchill played a large part in the **social reforms** of the Liberal government before **World War I.** These reforms—

such as improving conditions in the coal-mining industry and for household workers, and creating **pensions** for old people—were all part of turning Britain into a better place for working people. They also paved the way for later reforms, such as the creation of the National Health Service.

◀ *Churchill is pictured here in uniform as a young man during the Boer War, 1899–1902.*

World War I

Churchill is remembered mainly for the failure of the Gallipoli campaign in World War I—for which he was only partially responsible. Many people feel he should be remembered more for striving to find an alternative way of winning the war, instead of throwing more and more men into the machine guns, barbed wire, and artillery on the **Western Front.** Apart from trying to outflank the Germans with a landing at Gallipoli, he supported the development of such weaponry as tanks to protect soldiers on the front line.

Writing

Churchill proved to be a great **journalist** and writer. In the 1930s, he finished his four-volume work on the life of the Duke of Marlborough (Churchill's ancestor and a military leader in the eighteenth century), called *Marlborough, His Life and Times.* He also worked on *The History of the English-Speaking Peoples,* which was to be a best-selling history book in several volumes. Between 1948 and 1953, he wrote *The Second World War,* for which he was awarded the **Nobel Prize** for literature.

"His own man"

One of the accusations leveled at Churchill was that he changed political parties—not once, but twice. He started as a Conservative, disagreed with them, and went over to the Liberals. When he realized that the Liberals were a dying party in the 1920s, he went back to the Conservatives. This apparent lack of loyalty earned him many enemies. On the other hand, Churchill was always "his own man." Many people respect the fact that he refused to "toe the party line" (conform to the party's wishes) if he did not believe in the policies the party was following.

World War II

Churchill's great moment came in 1940. He said himself that he felt as if his whole life had been a preparation for him to lead Britain at one of the most dangerous times in its history, and this is what he is remembered for. He was decisive, and he gave inspired leadership to Britain. His speeches to the House of Commons and broadcasts to the nation are still remembered today. In the 1920s, the radio proved to be a wonderful invention for Churchill, because he could speak to everyone right in their own homes. No wartime leader had been able to do that before. He could reassure and unite people when bombs were falling on the cities, and when the news from the war fronts abroad was bad.

◀ *Prime Minister Winston Churchill inspects an American tommy gun during a 1940 tour of defenses along England's northeastern coast.*

At the end of World War II, the full horror of **Nazi** atrocities became known as the Allied soldiers reached the **concentration camps** where Jews and others who had opposed Hitler were held. People were horrified. Churchill was the symbol of the fact that the British people felt they had stood alone in 1940, refusing to give in to the great evil of Nazism.

During the war, Churchill was statesmanlike enough to bury his dislike and fear of **Communism,** and to have a working relationship with Britain's **ally,** the **Soviet Union.** He was also statesmanlike enough to build good working relationships with his wartime government. This included many men whose politics he did not like and some very powerful personalities who were not easy to work with.

Postwar Britain

In 1951, Churchill came back as a peacetime prime minister. He was becoming old and was a tired leader, but most people in Britain felt tired, too. The country needed time to recover quietly from six years of war.

Churchill could have been made a duke, but he always refused honors of that kind. Perhaps his greatest legacies were his beliefs in public service and **democracy.** He dedicated his life to the service of his country. When he was voted out of office in 1945, someone sympathized with him and said how ungrateful the British public was after all he had done. He retorted that the public had a right to vote him out of office. That was democracy, and that was what Britain had been fighting for.

Timeline

1874	Winston Leonard Spencer Churchill is born on November 30 at Blenheim Palace, Oxfordshire.
1894	Churchill joins the army. Churchill's father dies.
1895	Churchill goes to Cuba to observe the **civil war** there.
1897	In India, Churchill is involved in fighting and reporting on the Northwest Frontier. Churchill's first book, *The Malakand Field Force*, about the fighting in India, is published.
1898	In the Sudan, Churchill takes part in the cavalry charge at the Battle of Omdurman.
1899	Churchill writes a book about the campaign in the Sudan called *The River War*. In South Africa, while working as a **journalist** during the **Boer War**, Churchill is captured and escapes.
1900	Churchill fights in the Boer War and publishes his war notes called *London to Ladysmith*. Churchill enters Parliament as a Conservative **MP** for the town of Oldham in Lancashire.
1904	Churchill leaves the **Conservative Party** to join the **Liberal Party.**
1905	Churchill becomes Under Secretary of State for the **Colonies.**
1908	Churchill becomes President of the Board of Trade. Churchill marries Clementine Hozier.
1909	Churchill's first child, Diana, is born.
1910	Churchill becomes **Home Secretary.**
1911	His second child, Randolph, is born. Churchill becomes First Lord of the Admiralty.
1914	**World War I** begins. Churchill's third child, Sarah, is born.
1915	Churchill helps plan the attack on Gallipoli.
1916	Churchill fights as a soldier in the **trenches** on the **Western Front.**
1917	Churchill becomes Minister of **Munitions.**
1918	His fourth child, Marigold, is born. World War I ends.
1921	Churchill becomes Secretary for the Colonies. Churchill negotiates the treaty setting up the Irish Free State. Churchill's mother and daughter, Marigold, both die.

1922	His fifth child, Mary, is born.
	Churchill buys a country house—Chartwell in Kent.
1924	Churchill leaves the Liberal Party and joins the Conservative Party.
	Churchill becomes **Chancellor of the Exchequer.**
1925	Churchill puts Britain back onto the **Gold Standard.**
1926	Churchill organizes *The British Gazette* during the **General Strike** and works for a fair settlement of the coal miners' strike.
1929	Churchill is out of office but still an MP.
1930	Churchill writes an account of his life, so far called *My Early Life.*
1932	He spends a lot of time at Chartwell, painting, writing, and building walls.
1933	Churchill writes a book about his ancestor called *Marlborough, His Life and Times.*
1934	Churchill warns against the danger from **Nazi** Germany.
1939	**World War II** begins.
	Churchill becomes First Lord of the Admiralty.
1940	Churchill becomes prime minister.
	The evacuation at Dunkirk takes place.
	The Battle of Britain takes place.
1941	Germany invades the **Soviet Union.**
	The Japanese attack on Pearl Harbor, Hawaii, causes the U.S. to enter the war.
1942	The fall of Singapore takes place.
	The British gain a victory at El Alamein.
1943	The Allies invade Italy.
1944	The Allied invasion of Europe in Normandy (D-Day) takes place.
1945	Churchill, Roosevelt, and Stalin meet at Yalta.
	World War II comes to an end.
	Churchill is defeated in a general election.
1946	Churchill starts writing a book about World War II.
1951	Churchill wins the general election and becomes prime minister again.
1953	The coronation of Elizabeth II takes place.
	Churchill is awarded the **Nobel Prize** for literature for his book, *The Second World War.*
1955	Churchill retires from public life.
1956	Churchill finishes his last book, *A History of the English-Speaking Peoples.*
1965	Winston Churchill dies on January 24, at age 91. He is given a state funeral.

Key People of Churchill's Time

Eisenhower, General Dwight (1890–1969). Eisenhower was appointed the supreme commander of the Allied forces in 1944. He was the 34th president of the U.S. (1953–63).

Hitler, Adolf (1889–1945). Hitler helped to found the German **Nazi** Party, which came to power in 1933. He became the absolute ruler of Germany and worked to gain more land for his country, a policy which culminated in **World War II.** By 1945, Germany was defeated. Hitler committed suicide in May 1945.

Lenin, Vladimir Ilyich (1870–1924). Born Vladimir Ilyich Ulyanov, he took the name Lenin when he needed to hide because of his political activities. He studied the works of Karl Marx and founded the Bolshevik Party. In 1917, Lenin seized power in Russia following the fall of the czar (emperor), and worked to make Russia a **Communist** state.

Lloyd George, David (1863–1945). Lloyd George became a Member of Parliament in 1890. A great reformer who wanted a better life for working people, he became Minister of **Munitions** during **World War I,** then prime minister in 1916, at the age of 54.

Roosevelt, Franklin D. (1882–1945). Roosevelt was brought up believing he should serve the public. He was ready for a career in politics when he was struck down by polio at 38. He fought his way back to health, though was never able to walk again properly. He became president of the United States in 1933, and remained in office until his death.

Stalin, Joseph (1879–1953). Stalin took part in the Russian revolution of 1917, overthrowing the czar (emperor). He quickly rose to power alongside Lenin. When Lenin died in 1924, Stalin took control. For the next fifteen years he used ruthless methods to make Russia a more industrial country. Stalin fought Hitler with the **Allies,** but after 1945, relations between Stalin and the Allies deteriorated, ending in the **Cold War.** Stalin died on March 5, 1953.

The U.K. System of Government

The British system of government is a parliamentary democracy.

Parliament

Parliament consists of three parts: the monarch, the House of Lords, and the House of Commons.

The Monarch (King or Queen)

The monarchy has always been hereditary. This means when the monarch dies, his or her eldest son becomes king. If there are no sons, the eldest daughter becomes queen. The monarch must sign all new Acts of Parliament before they become law.

The House of Lords

Consists of **peers,** bishops (senior priests of the Church of England), and judges. Together they debate, or discuss, new laws and can ask for changes to be made.

The House of Commons

Consists of over 600 Members of Parliament (MPs), elected by the people of their **constituency** every 4 to 5 years. MPs propose, debate, and vote on new laws. The party with the most MPs in the House of Commons forms the government. The leader of this party becomes the prime minister.

A new law

A new law or bill is proposed by an MP, usually from the party in control, then debated and voted on by the House of Commons. If it is passed (wins a majority of votes), it is sent to the House of Lords, whose members then debate it and vote on it. If the bill is passed there, it is sent to the monarch, who signs it. This turns it into an Act of Parliament, and it is then law.

The real power rests with the elected House of Commons because they can overrule the House of Lords. No monarch has refused to sign a bill since Queen Anne in the eighteenth century.

Political parties

The main political parties in 1945 were the **Labour Party,** the **Conservative Party,** and the **Liberal Party.**

Sources for Further Research

Castor, H. *Winston Churchill*. Danbury, Conn.: Franklin Watts, 2000.

Churchill, Winston S. *Memoirs of the Second World War*. New York, N.Y.: Houghton Mifflin, 1991.

Downing, David. *Joseph Stalin*. Chicago: Heinemann Library, 2001.

Driemen, John E. *Winston Churchill: An Unbreakable Spirit*. Parsippany, N.J.: Silver Burdett Press, 1990.

Gilbert, Martin. *Churchill: A Life*. New York, N.Y.: Holt, Henry & Company, 1995.

Italia, Bob. *Winston Churchill*. Edina, Minn.: ABDO Publishing, 1990.

Lace, William W. *Winston Churchill*. San Diego, Calif.: Lucent Books, 1995.

Mansfield, Stephen. *Never Give in: The Extraordinary Character of Winston Churchill*. Elkton, Md.: Holly Hall Publications, 1995.

Reynoldson, Fiona. *Key Battles of World War II*. Chicago, Ill.: Heinemann Library, 2001.

Severance, John B. *Winston Churchill: Soldier, Statesman, Artist*. New York, N.Y.: Houghton Mifflin, 1996.

Taylor, David. *Adolf Hitler*. Chicago: Heinemann Library, 2001.

Taylor, David. *Franklin D. Roosevelt*. Chicago: Heinemann Library, 2001.

Taylor, Mike. *Leaders of World War II*. Edina, Minn.: ABDO Publishing, 1998.

Glossary

abdicate give up a position, usually a claim to the throne

alliance group of countries that fight together

allies group of countries that fight together; the Allies in World War II were England, Australia, New Zealand, France, and the United States

aristocratic describes someone who belongs to the wealthiest group in society, and who usually comes from a family of nobility

Boer white South African descended from the Dutch

Bolshevik Party one of the Communist political parties that emerged in Russia in 1903

British Empire group of countries around the world that were ruled by Britain; it started with a few colonies in the sixteenth century and reached its height in the nineteenth century

budget plan of spending drawn up by an individual or a government

Chancellor of the Exchequer senior member of the British government with responsibilities for the budget

civil war war where people of one country fight amongst themselves

coalition government made up of two or more political parties working together

Cold War period following World War II until the end of the 1980s, when the U.S. and the Soviet Union were enemies but never actually went to war

colony overseas territory controlled by a different country

commoner ordinary person

Commonwealth group of countries across the world that had formerly belonged to the British Empire

Communism political system in which everything is owned by the government and there is no private ownership of businesses

concentration camp prison camp for political prisoners. Concentration camps were used especially in Nazi Germany during World War II.

conciliatory describes the act of winning someone over to your side, often by making compromises

conscription process by which every man of fighting age has to join the armed forces

61

Conservative Party British political party that favors business interests

constituency area of the country represented by an MP; also refers to the people in that area

cryptographer someone who works with secret codes

death duty tax on money that is inherited from someone who has died

democracy system of government in which everybody has a chance to vote for a representative in government

dispatch message or report

DSO Distinguished Service Order, a medal awarded to soldiers for acts of bravery

economics subject relating to money, industry, and trade

Enigma machine machine for reading and writing in secret code used by the Germans in World War II

evacuate move to a safer place

export send goods out from a country

free election election in which all people are able to vote for whomever they wish

free trade buying and selling without taxes or restrictions

general election a vote that is held to elect the next government

General Strike event that took place in Britain in 1926 when the workers in all industries went on strike (stopped working) to demand better conditions

Gestapo Nazi secret police

Gold Standard system where a country's currency is backed by gold reserves

Home Rule right to self-government in Ireland

Home Secretary government minister responsible for affairs within the country

import bring goods into a country

journalist person who writes for newspapers, journals, and magazines

Labour Party British political party that aims to look after the welfare of working people

Liberal Party British political party that is interested in reform

maiden speech first speech an MP makes in the House of Commons

meningitis serious, sometimes fatal, illness where the lining of the brain becomes infected

MP Member of Parliament

munitions ammunition for guns

Nazi National Socialist German Workers' Party; also the name for people in this party (followers of Hitler)

Nobel Prize important prize awarded to people who have helped to make the world a better place

nutrition the elements in food that promote health and growth

orator skillful public speaker

peer person who holds a title such as lord or lady, either through inheritance or as an honor from the monarch

pension regular payment of money, often to someone who has retired from work

philosophy the study of ideas about life

pneumonia disease causing inflammation of the lungs

protectionism restrictions on trade designed to protect your own country's industries

shelled being shot at by artillery

social reform changing laws to make people's lives better

Soviet Union shortened name for the Union of Soviet Socialist Republics (USSR), formed in 1923 after the Communists had seized control

stock market place where stocks and shares of companies are bought and sold

trench long, narrow hole in the ground dug to protect soldiers

VC Victoria Cross, a medal awarded to members of the armed services for acts of bravery

war correspondent war reporter

welfare system system guaranteeing that everyone has enough money to live, a place to live, and access to health care and education

Western Front line of battle stretching from the north of France to the Swiss border in World War I

World War I war involving many countries of the world. It took place from 1914 to 1918, and was known as the Great War, until another world war began in 1939.

World War II second war involving many countries in the world. It took place from 1939 to 1945.

Index